Peanut Butter
Butter
Sweets

✳ ✳ ✳

Peanut Butter
Sweets

Pamela Bennett

GIBBS SMITH
TO ENRICH AND INSPIRE HUMANKIND

First Edition
16 15 14 13 12   5 4 3 2 1

Published by
Gibbs Smith
P.O. Box 667
Layton, Utah 84041

1.800.835.4993 orders
www.gibbs-smith.com

Designed by Rita Sowins / Sowins Design
Printed and bound in China
Gibbs Smith books are printed on either recycled, 100% post-consumer waste, FSC-certified papers or on paper produced from sustainable PEFC-certified forest/controlled wood source. Learn more at www.pefc.org.

Library of Congress Cataloging-in-Publication Data

Bennett, Pamela.
  Peanut butter sweets / Pamela Bennett ; photographs by Joyce Oudkerk Pool. — 1st ed.
     p. cm.
  Includes index.
  ISBN 978-1-4236-2448-6
1. Cooking (Peanut butter) 2. Desserts. 3. Confectionery. I. Title.
  TX814.5.P38B46 2012
  641.3'56596—dc23
                              2011038364

To all Bennett and Draughon family members;
what a blessed journey we've shared.

Acknowledgments

Michelle Branson and Joyce Oudkerk Pool; artists who encourage me to reach out and catch my star . . .

Introduction

Peanut butter was an "essential" in my mama's kitchen cupboard. It was woven into the everyday fabric of our lives: creamy peanut butter tucked inside hot buttermilk biscuits or generously slathered on bread with homemade blackberry jam, and the unmistakable fragrance of peanut butter cookies, fresh from the oven, awaiting us as we came home from school. Even when our mother became a successful business owner, she literally tucked a small jar of peanut butter in her purse everyday—it was her snack of choice. Growing up with peanut butter as a staple, it was only natural that my fifth-grade research project was written on the history of peanuts!

Peanuts were first grown by the Incas in Peru around 950 BC. They gradually made their way from South America to Africa and then onward to Spain, before finding their way to the American colonies. My native North Carolina shows a history of peanuts being planted by the year 1818, although some farmers claim that peanuts were growing there during the Revolutionary War.

George Washington Carver, the great botanist and inventor, promoted planting peanut crops to help poor farmers when their cotton crops failed. He developed over 100 recipes using peanuts as well as developing dyes, paints, cosmetics, even nitroglycerin using the complex, versatile peanut. His scientific research illuminated what we know today—peanuts are packed with protein and vitamins E and B3; they're higher in antioxidants than apples or carrots. However, the most important thing is—peanut butter just tastes delicious! It enhances whatever it accompanies. Scientists extol the health benefits of eating peanut butter, but the kitchen of my childhood elevated simple peanut butter treats to rock-star status.

The paradox seems to be that the more we eat peanut butter, the more we enjoy it. Its versatility allows us to never tire of it—perfect peanut butter bars, dreamy, creamy peanut butter pie, decadently rich penuche and fudge, gooey lip-smacking pound cake laced with thick peanut butter frosting . . . , so it's little wonder that the average American consumer eats six pounds of peanut butter each year. By the time a teen graduates from high school, she or he has eaten over 1,500 peanut butter sandwiches!

But there's so much more versatility and potential waiting inside each of these legumes. This book will guide you through simple steps, using basic ingredients, to produce amazing goodies. It is filled with mouth-watering recipes of delectable sweet treats featuring peanut butter as the star ingredient: cakes, pies, cookies, candies, toppings, beverages—amazing sweets that you can't imagine how you lived without before now.

Smoothies & Shakes

Peanut Butter
Smoothie

* *Makes 1-2 servings* *

¼ cup peanut butter

1 medium banana, peeled

2 tablespoons powdered creamer

1 (12-ounce) can Sprite

¾ to 1 cup ice

Combine all ingredients in a blender and blend until smooth.

Chocolate-
Peanut Butter Smoothie

✻ *Makes 2 servings* ✻

1 cup peanut butter
1 small avocado, ripe but not bruised in any way or overripe
2 cups soy milk
1 cup chocolate chips
2 tablespoons agave*
1½ cups ice

Combine and mix in a blender. The surprise is the avocado! It helps create a truly smooth smoothie.

*Agave is a plant-based sweetener. You can substitute honey.

Peanut Butter and
Banana Smoothie

* *Makes 2 servings* *

2 ripe frozen bananas*
2 cups almond milk
½ cup peanut butter

2 tablespoons agave**
¼ teaspoon vanilla
1 cup ice

Combine all ingredients in a blender and blend until the ice is well crushed, or if you prefer, blended until smooth.

*Freezing the bananas makes the smoothie much creamier.

**Agave is a plant-based sweetener. You can substitute honey.

Tropical
Smoothie

✳ *Makes 1-2 servings* ✳

⅓ cup peanut butter

1 large orange, peeled and segmented

2 cups banana slices

1 cup strawberries, cherries, or mango or papaya slices

1 cup soy or rice milk, divided

2 teaspoons agave*

½ cup ice

Combine peanut butter, fruit, half of the milk, and the agave in a blender. Process until smooth. Add the ice and continue processing until smooth. Add the remaining milk, if you desire a thinner consistency.

*Agave is a plant-based sweetener. You can substitute honey.

Quick Peanut Butter
Milkshake

* *Makes 2 servings* *

¾ cup vanilla ice cream
1 tablespoon sugar
4 tablespoons peanut butter

¼ cup milk
¼ cup Reese's Pieces candies
⅓ cup ice

Combine all ingredients in a blender. Pulse on low so ice breaks up, but do not over-process.

Egg-less Nog

1 quart vanilla-flavored soy milk

6 ounces extra firm silken tofu

4 tablespoons peanut butter

6 tablespoons maple syrup

2 tablespoons vanilla

2 teaspoons cinnamon

½ teaspoon nutmeg

¼ teaspoon ground cloves

Combine everything in a blender and process until creamy and smooth. Chill before serving.

Sprinkle cinnamon and nutmeg on top before serving in festive holiday glasses.

Southern Belle
Shake

✳ Makes 2 servings ✳

6 Reese's Peanut Butter Cups
2 cups milk

3 cups chocolate ice cream
1 (7-ounce) can Reddi-Whip

Process the first 3 ingredients in a blender until smooth. Top with a generous dollop of Reddi-Whip.

Sizzlin'
Milkshake

✱ *Makes 2 servings* ✱

3 cups vanilla ice cream

½ cup peanut butter

½ cup red cinnamon candies

1 heaping tablespoon cayenne pepper

1 teaspoon vanilla*

1 cup ice

¼ teaspoon cocoa, sweetened or unsweetened, as desired

Combine all ingredients except the cocoa. Blend in a blender until creamy. Dust the top of the shakes with the cocoa.

*Authentic Mexican vanilla preferred.

Float Your Boat

4 scoops apple pie ice cream
½ cup peanut butter
1 teaspoon nutmeg

1 teaspoon cinnamon
2 cups sparkling apple cider

Place 2 scoops of ice cream in each of 2 tall sundae glasses. Combine the peanut butter, nutmeg, and cinnamon and spoon over the ice cream. Pour the apple cider over the top. Serve with tall straws and spoons. This is especially good on a crisp autumn day.

Rootin' Tootin'
Float

✱ *Makes 4 servings* ✱

4 scoops vanilla ice cream

½ cup crunchy peanut butter

1 teaspoon vanilla

2 (12-ounce) cans root beer

12 vanilla wafers, crushed

4 sticks cinnamon

Scoop the ice cream into 4 glasses. Evenly divide the peanut butter among the glasses and place on top of the ice cream. Add the vanilla to the root beer and pour over the ice cream.

Sprinkle the crushed wafers over the top of the floats. Finish with a cinnamon stick to stir the float.

Cookies, Bars, & Muffins

Beach Balls

12 or more Oreo cookies

1 cup peanut butter

¼ cup butter or margarine, softened

¼ cup dry powdered milk

12 or more Pecan Sandies cookies

Place all of the Oreo cookies in a large ziplock baggie and smash them with a rolling pin or hammer. You want recognizable bits, so do not pulverize to crumbs.

In a large bowl, combine the peanut butter, butter, and powdered milk. Add the crushed Oreos to this mix. When well blended, roll this mixture by hand into golf ball-size balls. Set aside.

Place all of the Pecan Sandies in a separate ziplock baggie and smash them. In this case, you want the final result to look like sand on the beach—no visible chunks—just a fine, pulverized product.

Roll the balls in the Pecan Sandies "sand" and refrigerate for an hour before serving.

Quickie Peanut Butter
Cookies

✳ *Makes 2 dozen cookies* ✳

2½ cups quick oats

2 cups peanut butter

1 teaspoon vanilla

2 cups butter or margarine

2 cups milk

4 tablespoons cocoa powder, sweetened or unsweetened, as desired

2 cups sugar

Place the oats, peanut butter, and vanilla in a large bowl. In a medium saucepan, heat the remaining ingredients and boil for about 2 minutes.

Pour the hot mixture over the contents of the bowl. Thoroughly mix together and drop by teaspoonful on waxed paper. Allow to cool before eating.

Polar Bears

✷ *Makes 2 dozen balls* ✷

1 cup crunchy peanut butter

1 cup dry powdered milk

1 cup honey

1 teaspoon vanilla

8 ounces white chocolate

1/4 cup vegetable shortening

1 cup shredded coconut

In a large bowl, mix the peanut butter, powdered milk, honey, and vanilla. Blend well with flat spatula. Roll around by hand and shape into golf ball-size balls. Set aside.

In a medium microwave-safe bowl, melt white chocolate and shortening together in microwave until smooth. Cook on a low setting in increments of 30 seconds. Check after every 30 seconds to prevent overcooking. Stir to blend thoroughly after each microwave time.

Using kitchen tongs, dip each ball individually into the white chocolate mixture to cover completely.

Roll the balls around a plate sprinkled with coconut, covering each one completely. Place on waxed paper and allow to set for about 30 minutes before eating.

Five-Ingredient
Peanut Butter Cookies

❋ Makes 2 dozen cookies ❋

¾ cup peanut butter

1 (14-ounce) can sweetened
   condensed milk

2 cups Bisquick

1 teaspoon vanilla

¼ cup brown sugar

Preheat oven to 375 degrees.

In a large bowl, whisk peanut butter and milk until smooth.

Add the Bisquick and vanilla to the peanut butter mixture. Blend together until ingredients are well distributed. Using your hands, shape dough into 1-inch balls. Sprinkle the brown sugar on a plate and roll the balls in the sugar to cover.

On an ungreased baking sheet, flatten the cookies using a spoon or your hand, and bake for approximately 5–7 minutes.

Cry Baby
Cookies

1 cup sugar, divided

¼ cup peanut butter

¾ cup vegetable shortening

1 large egg

2 cups flour

2 tablespoons molasses

2 teaspoons baking soda

2 teaspoons ginger powder

1 teaspoon cinnamon

¼ teaspoon salt

Preheat oven to 375 degrees.

Reserve ¼ cup of the sugar. Mix all of the other ingredients together in large bowl. Roll dough into 1-inch balls. Sprinkle the reserved sugar on a plate and roll the balls in sugar until covered. Place on an ungreased baking sheet in ball form or flatten with your hand or a spoon and bake for 20 minutes.

Little Helper
Peanut Butter Cookies

1 cup peanut butter
1 cup sugar

1 small egg
1 teaspoon vanilla

Preheat oven to 325 degrees.

In a large bowl, combine all ingredients and drop by tablespoonful on an ungreased cookie sheet. Bake for 15 minutes.

This is a great recipe for making with small children. It is messy, but fun!

Potato Chip
Cookies

½ cup crunchy peanut butter
½ cup butter or margarine
3 cups flour
1 cup sugar

1 teaspoon vanilla
1 cup crushed potato chips
1 cup powdered sugar

Preheat oven to 350 degrees.

In a large bowl, cream the peanut butter and butter then mix in the flour, sugar, and vanilla; thoroughly combine. Add the crushed potato chips to this mixture.

Form mixture into golf ball-size balls. Place on an ungreased baking sheet and bake for 15 minutes. Cool the cookies then dust with powdered sugar.

Peanut Butter
Macaroons

✳ *Makes 2 dozen cookies* ✳

1 (16-ounce) bag shredded coconut

1 (14-ounce) can sweetened
   condensed milk

⅓ cup peanut butter

2 teaspoons vanilla

Preheat oven to 350 degrees.

Mix all ingredients in a large bowl then drop by teaspoonful on a greased baking sheet. Bake for 10 minutes.

No-Bake
Wonders

✽ *Makes 16–20 bars* ✽

1 cup raisins

1 cup pitted dates

1/2 cup candied cherries

1 cup whole peanuts

1/2 cup crunchy peanut butter

3 tablespoons orange juice

1/2 to 3/4 cup powdered sugar

In a large bowl, mix all ingredients together, except powdered sugar, adding orange juice as the final step to blend. If too dry, add more juice 1 tablespoon at a time.

Press by hand in a greased 8 x 8-inch pan. Sift the powdered sugar on top. Chill overnight. Cut into bars.

Yummy Peanut
Squares

✶ *Makes 3 dozen squares* ✶

Squares

2 cups graham cracker crumbs

2 tablespoons brown sugar

1/2 cup melted butter or margarine

1 (14-ounce) can sweetened condensed milk

1 (7-ounce) package shredded coconut

2 teaspoons vanilla

Topping

1 (6-ounce) package peanut butter morsels

1 (6-ounce) package butterscotch morsels

8 tablespoons crunchy peanut butter

5 tablespoons butter

1/2 cup chopped peanuts

Preheat oven to 325 degrees.

In a large bowl, combine the graham cracker crumbs, brown sugar, and butter. Pat mixture in a greased 9 x 13-inch baking pan. Bake for 10 minutes. Set aside and allow to cool for 15 or more minutes.

Combine the condensed milk, coconut, and vanilla in a large bowl and pour over the baked crust. Return to oven and bake for 25 minutes more. Allow to cool again.

In a large microwave-safe bowl, melt all of the topping ingredients except for peanuts in microwave on medium setting for 3 minutes, stopping the microwave at each minute interval to stir and blend the mixture. Don't overcook. Spread this mixture over the top of the baked squares, sprinkle peanuts over top, and allow to cool before cutting.

Peanut Butter
Bars

✳ *Makes 24 bars* ✳

1 cup sugar

1 cup corn syrup

1½ cups crunchy peanut butter

3 cups corn flakes

1 (12-ounce) package butterscotch chips

In a medium saucepan, bring sugar and corn syrup to boil. Stir in peanut butter then remove from heat. Pour over the corn flakes in a large bowl. Blend these ingredients and transfer into a greased 9 x 9-inch pan. Evenly spread the mixture in the pan and press, using hands or a spatula.

In a large microwave-safe bowl, melt the butterscotch chips in microwave, or melt in a medium saucepan over low heat on the stove top. Pour the melted butterscotch over the cereal mix. Allow to cool. Cut into small bars when mixture is set.

Chewies

1 (3.5-ounce) package dry cook and serve vanilla or chocolate pudding mix

½ cup light corn syrup

½ cup peanut butter

4 cups dry cereal (Rice Krispies or Chex works well)

Prepare a 9 x 9-inch pan with nonstick cooking spray and set aside.

Combine the pudding mix and corn syrup in a large saucepan. Allow to reach a low boil, about 2 minutes. Stir continuously. Remove from heat, blend in the peanut butter, and mix well. Add the cereal. Stir to coat.

Pour mixture in prepared pan and cool for about 30 minutes before cutting.

Peanut Butter
Oatmeal Bars

❋ Makes 3 dozen bars ❋

½ cup butter or margarine
½ cup sugar
½ cup brown sugar
½ cup dark corn syrup

2 tablespoons vanilla
4 cups quick oats
⅔ cup crunchy peanut butter
1 (6-ounce) package chocolate chips

Preheat oven to 350 degrees and prepare a 9 x 13-inch pan with nonstick cooking spray.

In a large bowl, cream the butter and sugars then stir in the corn syrup and vanilla. Add the oatmeal and thoroughly combine. Using a spatula, spread mixture into the prepared pan. Bake for 15 minutes.

While cookies are baking, melt the peanut butter and chocolate chips in a medium microwave-safe bowl in the microwave. When the cookies have slightly cooled, pour the peanut butter mixture over the top. Chill for at least 1 hour before cutting into bars.

P.B. & J.
Bars

✱ *Makes 24-30 bars* ✱

1 cup butter
1½ cups sugar
2½ cups peanut butter
2 large eggs
2 teaspoons vanilla

3 cups flour
1 teaspoon baking powder
2 teaspoons salt
2 cups jam, of choice

Preheat oven to 350 degrees and grease a 9 x 13-inch pan.

With an electric mixer, beat the butter and sugar together in a large bowl for about 2 minutes. Add the peanut butter, eggs, and vanilla and beat 2 minutes more.

In a medium bowl, combine the flour, baking powder, and salt. Add to the peanut butter mixture in increments, using a low speed. Combine well.

Pour slightly more than half of the batter in prepared pan. Spread the jam over this mixture and spoon the remaining peanut butter batter on top of the jam.

Bake for 35–40 minutes. When cool, cut into bars.

Peanut
Coconut Muffins

✷ Makes 24 muffins ✷

2 cups sugar

½ cup water

6 medium eggs

1 cup flour

3 tablespoons butter

½ cup peanut butter

1½ cups shredded coconut

Preheat oven to 350 degrees and prepare muffin tins with nonstick cooking spray or paper liners.

In a medium saucepan, boil the sugar in the water. Stir constantly until a syrup-like consistency has been reached. Remove from heat.

Transfer to a medium bowl and slowly add the eggs, slightly beating after each is added. Mix on low speed with electric hand mixer. Add the flour, butter, peanut butter, and coconut. Blend well after each ingredient.

Fill muffin cups ⅔ full and bake for 20 minutes.

Peanut Butter
Muffins

2 cups flour
½ cup sugar
2½ teaspoons baking powder
½ teaspoon salt

½ cup peanut butter
2 tablespoons butter or margarine
1 cup milk
2 small eggs

Preheat oven to 400 degrees. Prepare a muffin tin with nonstick cooking spray or paper liners.

Sift dry ingredients together in a large bowl. Cut in the peanut butter along with the butter and blend until it resembles coarse crumbles. Add the milk and eggs all at once and stir well.

Fill muffin cups ⅔ full and bake for 15 minutes. Makes 12 large muffins

Variation: You can use a mini muffin pan following the above directions. Check on muffins after 10-12 minutes of baking time.

Cakes & Pies

Peanut Butter
Pound Cake

✳ Makes 12 servings ✳

Cake

3 cups sifted flour
1 teaspoon baking powder
2 teaspoons salt
¼ cup butter, softened
1 cup peanut butter
3 cups sugar

5 eggs
2 teaspoons vanilla

Frosting

1½ cups powdered sugar
¼ cup milk
¼ cup peanut butter
2 tablespoons vanilla

Preheat oven to 325 degrees. Grease a tube or Bundt pan.

In a medium bowl, combine flour, baking powder, and salt; set aside.

In a large bowl, beat butter and peanut butter until smooth using electric mixer. Add sugar and continue mixing until smooth, about 4 minutes. Add the eggs, one at a time, mixing thoroughly after each addition. Stir in the vanilla and gradually add the flour to the peanut butter mixture.

Pour batter into prepared pan and bake for 1 hour and 20 minutes. Allow cake to cool.

In a medium bowl, combine frosting ingredients until smooth. Frost cake.

Peanut Butter
Malted Cake

1 box chocolate cake mix

1/3 cup peanut butter

6 tablespoons powdered malted milk or crushed malted milk ball candies

1/2 to 1 cup powdered sugar

Preheat oven to 350 degrees. Grease a Bundt pan.

In a large bowl, prepare the cake following the box directions, adding the peanut butter and malted milk powder or malted milk candies to the mix; stir well.

Bake according to the box directions, using Bundt pan instructions. When cake has cooled, sprinkle the powdered sugar over top and sides of the cake.

Peanut Butter and
Jelly Cake

✱ *Makes 8 servings* ✱

1 box yellow cake mix

¾ to 1 cup jam, of choice

1 (10-ounce) package peanut butter chips

4 to 5 tablespoons milk

1 (16-ounce) container vanilla frosting

Preheat oven to 350 degrees.

Bake the cake in 2 round pans according to box directions. When cool, cut the cakes in half horizontally. Spread the jam on top of 3 layers, but not the top layer. Stack and create a 4-layer cake.

In a small saucepan, combine the peanut butter chips and milk, melting and stirring over medium-low heat until smooth. Remove from heat and combine this mixture with the frosting in a large bowl. Beat until thoroughly combined. Spread this icing over the top and sides of the cake.

Peanut Butter
Cheesecake

Cheesecake

1 (9-inch) graham cracker pie crust

½ cup peanut butter

16 ounces cream cheese

3 eggs

¾ cup sugar

2 tablespoons vanilla

Topping

1 cup sour cream

¼ cup sugar

3 tablespoons peanut butter

1 tablespoon vanilla

Preheat oven to 350 degrees.

In a large bowl, beat the peanut butter, cream cheese, and eggs together. When all lumps are gone, add the sugar and vanilla. Mix well. Pour into the graham cracker crust and bake for 30 minutes.

While cheesecake is baking, combine the topping ingredients in a medium bowl and set aside. Spread the topping over the cheesecake while still warm. Turn the oven temperature to 400 degrees and return the cheesecake to the oven for 5 additional minutes. Cool completely, then refrigerate.

Luscious
Lava Cake

5 ounces semisweet chocolate, chopped

¼ cup unsalted butter

2 large eggs

2 large egg yolks

6 tablespoons sugar

2 teaspoons vanilla

4 tablespoons peanut butter

1 teaspoon salt

2 tablespoons flour

Preheat oven to 400 degrees and grease 4 custard or soufflé cups. Place on a baking sheet with sides.

Stir the chocolate and butter together in a small saucepan over low heat until smooth. Remove from heat and allow to cool 10 minutes. Stir occasionally.

Using an electric mixer, beat the eggs plus egg yolks, sugar, vanilla, peanut butter, and salt in a medium bowl. When a thick "ribbon" cascades from the mixer, about 5–6 minutes, you can then fold in the flour. Stir to incorporate. Gently fold in the chocolate mixture.

Spoon the batter into the prepared custard cups and bake for 15 minutes. The top of each cake will be soft and dry, while the interior will be moist. When you spoon into this beauty, the "lava" will ooze out.

Mud Slide

Makes 8 servings

1 box German chocolate cake mix

1 (12-ounce) can sweetened
  condensed milk

1 cup peanut butter

1 (4.5-ounce) container German
  chocolate frosting

Prepare the cake mix following box instructions using a 9 x 13-inch pan.

While the cake is still warm, poke holes throughout the top of the cake using a plastic straw or skewer. Pour the condensed milk into these holes.

Combine the peanut butter and frosting in a medium microwave-safe bowl and microwave until warm. Pour this combination all over the top and sides of the cake. Refrigerate overnight before serving.

Deep South
Peanut Butter Pie

1 (9-inch) refrigerated pie crust
1/2 cup peanut butter
2 large eggs
1/3 cup Bisquick
1/4 cup sugar
1/2 cup brown sugar

1/4 cup corn syrup
2 teaspoons vanilla
1/2 teaspoon cinnamon
Dash salt
1 1/4 cups chopped peanuts
1 cup whipped cream topping

Preheat oven to 350 degrees.

Bake the pie crust according to directions on label. Allow to cool while processing the remaining ingredients.

Combine the peanut butter, eggs, Bisquick, sugars, and corn syrup in a blender and process until smooth, about 2 minutes. Add the vanilla, cinnamon, and salt and process for an additional 10–15 seconds.

Sprinkle the peanuts into the bottom of the baked pie shell and pour the liquid mixture over the entire pie. Bake for 45–55 minutes.

When pie has cooled, spread the whipped topping over the pie.

My Oh My,
Peanut Butter Pie

* *Makes 6 servings* *

1 cup crunchy peanut butter

8 ounces cream cheese, softened

1 cup sugar

2 tablespoons butter or margarine

1 tablespoon vanilla

1 (9-inch) graham cracker pie crust

1 cup whipped topping

⅓ cup caramel topping

Using an electric mixer, beat the peanut butter, cream cheese, sugar, butter, and vanilla together in a large bowl. Pour mixture into the graham cracker crust. Chill overnight.

The next day, use a spatula to gently cover the top of the pie with the whipped topping. Warm the caramel topping in a microwave, stirring at 15-second intervals until pourable. Be careful not to burn. Swirl or drip the warmed caramel on top of the whipped topping before serving.

Peanut Butter
Vanilla Pie

1 (9-inch) refrigerated pie shell

1 (3.5-ounce) package instant vanilla pudding mix

1½ cups milk

1½ cup walnuts or pecans, halves or pieces

½ cup peanut butter

½ teaspoon cinnamon

3 tablespoons powdered malted milk

Bake the pie shell according to the package directions. Set aside.

Prepare the pudding with the milk following package directions in a large bowl. Add the remaining ingredients to the pudding. Blend well and pour into the baked pie shell. Chill before serving.

Faux
Moo Pie

✳ *Makes 6-8 servings* ✳

1 (12-ounce) package vegan
chocolate chips

16 ounces firm tofu

1½ cups peanut butter

¼ cup soy milk

1 (9-inch) graham cracker crust

1 cup chopped nuts, of choice

In a medium microwave-safe bowl, melt vegan chocolate chips in microwave.

In a food processor or blender, add the melted chocolate, tofu, peanut butter, and soy milk. Blend until smooth. Stir in the chopped nuts. Pour into graham cracker crust. Refrigerate 2–3 hours.

Variation: If you desire a hard topping, make and chill the pie as directed. Melt 1 additional cup of chocolate chips and pour over top of the pie. Refrigerate again for 2–3 more hours.

Heath Bar
Pie

12 (1.4-ounce) Heath Bars
⅓ cup crunchy peanut butter
1 pint whipping cream

2 teaspoons sugar
1 teaspoon vanilla
1 (9-inch) graham cracker pie crust

Crush the Heath bars in their wrappers with a hammer or rolling pin. Discard wrappers and add these bars to the crunchy peanut butter in a medium bowl. Blend well and set aside.

In a large bowl using an electric mixer, whip the cream until very stiff, gradually adding the sugar. Fold the vanilla into this mix. Blend the cream mixture into the peanut butter mixture.

Pour into the graham cracker crust and refrigerate 6 or more hours.

Peanut Butter
Chess Pie

⅓ cup peanut butter

1 cup sugar

3 tablespoons cornmeal

3 tablespoons sweetened cocoa

3 medium eggs

½ cup butter, melted

½ cup corn syrup

2 teaspoons vanilla

1 (9-inch) unbaked pie shell

Preheat oven to 350 degrees.

In a large bowl, stir the peanut butter, sugar, cornmeal, and cocoa together until well blended. In a medium bowl, combine the eggs, butter, corn syrup, and vanilla. Beat well and add to the first mixture. Stir until smooth.

Pour mixture in the unbaked pie shell. Bake for 45 minutes or until the middle has set.

Fluffy Dream
Pie

1 (9-inch) pie shell

2 (2.6-ounce) envelopes Dream Whip topping mix

2¾ cups milk, divided

2 (4-ounce) packages vanilla instant pudding or pie mix

½ cup smooth peanut butter

Bake the pie shell according to the package directions and set aside.

Prepare the whipped topping mix using 1 cup of the milk in a large bowl.

Add the remaining milk to the pudding mix and peanut butter in a separate large bowl. Stir until a smooth consistency is reached.

Combine the whipped topping with the pudding mixture. Blend by using an electric mixer on high speed for 2 minutes. Pour into the baked pie shell. Chill for at least 4 hours before serving.

Desserts & Treats

Party
Poppers

1/3 cup peanut butter

3 tablespoons butter or margarine, softened

3 tablespoons corn syrup

1 tablespoon orange zest

1 tablespoon vanilla

1/2 teaspoon salt

2 cups powdered sugar

1 pound pecan or walnut halves

3 pounds large pitted dates

In a large mixing bowl, cream the peanut butter and butter together. Add the corn syrup, orange zest, vanilla, and salt. Mix well. Stir in all of the powdered sugar. After blending completely, mix with your hands. Move this mixture to a board on your countertop. Knead the mixture until it becomes cohesive.

Wrap in aluminum foil or plastic wrap and refrigerate. Chill for at least 4 hours, or overnight.

Remove mixture from refrigerator. Wrap 1/2–1 teaspoon of the mixture around a pecan or walnut half. Stuff a coated nut into each of the dates.

Peanut Butter and
Apple Cobbler

✱ *Makes 4 servings* ✱

1 (20-ounce) can apple pie filling

½ cup peanut butter

½ cup Bisquick

3 tablespoons butter or margarine

½ cup milk

⅔ cup sugar

½ cup walnut or pecan halves

Preheat oven to 375 degrees.

Spoon the apple pie filling in bottom of a 9 x 9-inch baking dish.

Combine all ingredients, except the nuts, into a blender and blend for 1 minute. Pour blended ingredients over the top of the apple filling. Drop all the nuts on top of the batter. Don't stir! The magic occurs without it. Bake for 30 minutes.

Homemade Peanut Butter
Ice Cream

4 cups half-and-half

3 cups dry powdered milk

3 cups milk

1½ cups peanut butter

1½ cups sugar

4 teaspoons vanilla

In a large saucepan, combine half-and-half, powdered milk, and milk. Cook over low heat until granules have dissolved. Add the peanut butter and sugar and continue cooking until smooth, about 4 minutes. Add the vanilla and remove from heat.

Allow to cool before refrigerating until chilled. When completely cooled, add mixture to an ice cream freezer and follow the directions for your freezer model.

Peanut Butter
Turnovers

2 cups peanut butter

½ cup peanut butter chips

1 cup chopped macadamia nuts

1 (17-ounce) package frozen puff pastry

1 medium egg, lightly whisked

Preheat oven to 400 degrees.

In a medium bowl, combine peanut butter, peanut butter chips, and macadamia nuts. Set aside.

Unroll the puff pastry on a floured surface and cut into 12–16 equal-size squares. Place one teaspoon filling on each pastry piece. Fold on the diagonal to create a triangle shape. Press any edges closed.

Brush the tops of each triangle with the egg. Place turnovers on a baking sheet and bake for 15 minutes.

Igloo Bombe

2 pints Homemade Peanut Butter
  Ice Cream (see page 80)

2 pints caramel swirl ice cream

12 small-size chocolate candy bars,
  chopped to make 1 cup

10 to 12 peanut butter cookies,
  crushed

1 (7-ounce) bottle peanut butter
  and chocolate shell ice cream
  topping

Prepare a large bowl with nonstick cooking spray and line with plastic wrap; overlap halfway on the outside of the bowl.

Remove Homemade Peanut Butter Ice Cream from freezer container or cut carton away from purchased 2-pint containers. Cut the ice cream into rounds, 2-inches wide by 1-inch thick, using a metal cookie or biscuit cutter. Place these slices into the bowl, covering the bottom and side, leaving room at the top. Fill in gaps with ice cream using a spatula. Freeze for 30 minutes.

Soften the caramel ice cream. Stir to soften evenly and mix in chopped candy. Spoon the caramel ice cream into the bowl and spread evenly. Sprinkle cookie crumbs over the top and press down into the ice cream. Fold plastic wrap over the top to cover and freeze overnight.

To prepare for serving: cut a paper plate to fit. Invert the bombe onto the paper plate. Remove the bowl and plastic wrap. Smooth over any unsightly spots. Pour the shell ice cream topping onto the bombe and spread it evenly with a spatula. Place on a serving plate and return to freezer until time to serve. This can be stored for up to 1 week.

Peanut Butter
Cups

✱ *Makes 36 cups* ✱

36 miniature Reese's Peanut Butter Cup candies

1 (14-ounce) package refrigerated peanut butter cookie dough

Preheat oven to 350 degrees. Refrigerate candy for about 30 minutes prior to making recipe and unwrap before using. Prepare miniature muffin tins with nonstick cooking spray.

Slice the cookie dough into quarters. Place a quarter slice of dough into each muffin cup. Bake 8-10 minutes. Remove from oven and quickly push one candy deeply into each individual muffin cup. Heat from the dough will allow the cookie to rise above the candy.

Cool and then refrigerate for about 30 minutes before serving.

Peanut Butter
Soufflé

❋ *Makes 4 servings* ❋

⅓ cup whipping cream

1 (3-ounce) package cream cheese

½ cup peanut butter

½ cup chocolate pieces, semi-dark
   or milk chocolate

3 medium eggs, separated

Dash salt

½ cup powdered sugar

Preheat oven to 300 degrees.

Blend the cream and cream cheese in a medium heavy saucepan over low heat. Add the peanut butter and chocolate pieces and stir until melted. Take care not to scorch.

Remove mixture from the stove and allow to cool. Meanwhile, in a small bowl, beat the egg yolks with salt until thickened, about 5 minutes. Blend this into the cooled peanut butter mixture.

In a large bowl, beat the egg whites until soft peaks have formed. Gradually add the sugar and continue beating until stiff peaks form. Fold whites, a small amount at a time, into the peanut butter mixture.

Pour into an ungreased 1-quart soufflé dish and bake for 50 minutes. If preparing in individual ramekins, increase oven temperature to 325 degrees and bake for 15 minutes. Serve immediately.

Peanut Butter
Mousse

✳ *Makes 4 servings* ✳

1 (6-ounce) package peanut butter
  chips
¼ cup peanut butter

¼ cup butter
6 medium eggs, separated

Melt the peanut butter chips, peanut butter, and butter in a double boiler, stirring continuously so mixture doesn't stick. Add the egg yolks to the mixture. Keep stirring until completely incorporated. Reduce heat.

In a large bowl, beat the egg whites until they become stiff. Remove peanut butter mixture from the stove. Fold egg whites into the cooked mixture. Pour into individual serving parfait glasses or desert cups. Chill at least 4 hours before serving.

Peanut Butter
Banana Pops

4 medium bananas

½ cup creamy peanut butter

4 tablespoons honey

4 wooden skewers

shredded coconut

chopped peanuts

cookie sprinkles

chocolate chips

crushed candies

Peel bananas; set aside. Combine the peanut butter with honey in a small microwave-safe bowl and microwave until warm, about 1 minute. Set aside.

Run skewer through each banana. Place peanut butter mixture on a plate and sprinkle each individual topping on separate plates. Roll each banana in peanut butter mixture then coat with favorite toppings from the individual plates.

Place on waxed paper to eat within an hour or freeze for serving later that day. This treat is not intended to remain in freezer for more than 24 hours.

Swirlies

1 cup brown sugar
1/3 cup milk
1/4 cup light corn syrup
1 tablespoon butter or margarine

1/4 cup peanut butter
1 pint ice cream, vanilla, fudge ripple, cookies-and-cream, or Moose tracks
1/2 cup salted peanuts

Combine first 4 ingredients in a medium saucepan and cook on medium heat until sugar dissolves. Remove from heat, stir in the peanut butter, and keep stirring until smooth.

In 4 parfait or other tall glasses, alternate layers of ice cream and peanut butter mixture. Repeat layers. Sprinkle peanuts on top.

Hobo
S'mores

1 (12-ounce) jar peanut butter
12 saltine crackers
12 jumbo marshmallows

Preheat broiler.

Smear peanut butter on a cracker, place a marshmallow on top, and place on a baking sheet. Broil until marshmallow turns charred, runny, and oh so gooey! Check oven after 1 minute and watch carefully until marshmallows are just how you like them.

Cheesy
Peanut Butter Ball

1 (8-ounce) package cream cheese, softened

1 cup powdered sugar

3 to 4 tablespoons sugar

¾ cup crunchy peanut butter

1 (9-ounce) package peanut butter chips

Using a hand mixer, beat the cream cheese, sugars, and peanut butter until well-blended. Spoon onto plastic wrap, pull up all 4 corners, and twist into shape of a ball. Wrap in plastic wrap and freeze for 1½ hours.

Remove from freezer and press peanut butter chips into exterior of the ball. Cover and freeze 2 more hours before serving. Let stand at room temperature for about 15 minutes before serving.

Serve with crackers, small party biscuits, or fresh fruits.

Apple Hearts

✱ Makes 4 servings ✱

4 medium Red Delicious apples

1 cup crunchy peanut butter

2 teaspoons cinnamon

1 teaspoon ground nutmeg

½ cup Red Hots (cinnamon candies)

½ cup water

2 tablespoons butter or margarine

Preheat oven to 375 degrees.

Core the apples and remove and discard the center leaving a hollow section but with much of the meat of the apple still intact. Take care not to core through the bottom.

In a small bowl, mix the peanut butter with cinnamon and nutmeg and stuff into the apples. Leave enough room at the top of each apple to place a good amount of the Red Hots.

Pour water in bottom of a loaf pan and add butter. Stand the apples upright in the pan and bake for 30 minutes. The aroma alone will make you do a happy autumn dance!

Candies

Peanut Butter
Patties

2¼ cups sugar
⅔ cup corn syrup
1 cup evaporated milk
3 cups raw peanuts

1 tablespoon butter or margarine
⅓ cup peanut butter
1 tablespoon vanilla
Red food coloring

In a medium saucepan, combine the sugar, corn syrup, evaporated milk, and raw peanuts. Cook over medium heat at a slow boil, 235–240 degrees on a candy thermometer, for at least 45 minutes. Stir continuously. The consistency is correct when a drop of the cooked mixture forms into a ball when dropped into a bowl of cold water, or hard-ball stage.

After hard-ball stage has been reached, stir in the butter, peanut butter, vanilla, and 3–4 drops red food coloring. Incorporate well. Spoon patties on parchment or waxed paper to cool.

Peanut Butter
Fudge

2 cups sugar

²⁄₃ cup evaporated milk

½ cup margarine

1 (6-ounce) package chocolate chips

1 cup peanut butter

¾ cup chopped pecans

Bring sugar and evaporated milk to a full boil in a large saucepan. Stir constantly for exactly 6 minutes. Remove from heat and add margarine, chocolate chips, peanut butter, and pecans. Stir until thoroughly combined.

Pour into an 8 x 8-inch pan and refrigerate for at least 6 hours.

Penuche

2 cups sugar

1 pound brown sugar

¾ cup milk

12 ounces crunchy peanut butter

6 tablespoons marshmallow cream

2 tablespoons vanilla

In a large saucepan, combine both sugars with the milk. Boil for 3–4 minutes over medium heat. Add the peanut butter, marshmallow cream, and vanilla. Beat together until combined and smooth. Pour into a greased 9 x 9-inch pan. Allow to cool before cutting.

White Mints

1 pound white chocolate, broken into pieces

½ cup chunky peanut butter

2 to 3 drops peppermint flavoring, optional

⅔ cup mint chips

In a large microwave-safe bowl, microwave the white chocolate for about 5 minutes on a medium setting. Stir after each 1 minute of cooking to prevent scorching.

Add the peanut butter and stir until smooth, about 1 minute. Add the peppermint flavoring, if using. Spread in a 9 x 9-inch pan.

In a medium microwave-safe bowl, microwave the mint chips for about 2 minutes. Stir after 1 minute of cooking. Drizzle over the white chocolate mixture. Cool then cut into squares.

Lip Smackin'
Candy

* *Makes approximately 30 pieces* *

1 cup crunchy peanut butter

1 cup butter, softened

1 pound powdered sugar

1½ cups graham cracker crumbs

1 (12-ounce) package butterscotch chips

In a large bowl, blend peanut butter and butter until smooth. Add the powdered sugar and graham cracker crumbs and mix well. Press into a greased 9 x 13-inch pan; set aside.

Melt the butterscotch chips in a medium saucepan over medium heat. Stir often to prevent scorching. When completely melted, quickly spread over the peanut butter mixture.

Chill for at least 1 hour before cutting into small squares.

Pete's Peanut Butter
Pinwheels

2 pounds powdered sugar, divided

2 tablespoons butter or margarine, melted

¼ teaspoon vanilla

2 to 3 teaspoons milk

1 (12-ounce) jar smooth peanut butter

Reserve about ¼ cup of the powdered sugar to "flour" the dough roll to prevent it from sticking to your counter top or candy prep board.

Mix remainder of sugar, butter, and vanilla in a large bowl. Add milk in the smallest of increments, a few drops at a time. Be very careful to not use more milk than needed in order to mix these ingredients. This should resemble a dry loaf similar to bread dough. If too much milk is used, the mixture cannot be rolled out.

When ingredients are thoroughly mixed, sprinkle the reserved powdered sugar on your prep area. Use a rolling pin to roll the loaf into the shape of a flat pie crust, about ¼-inch thick.

Once the dough has been rolled to resemble a flat crust, use a table knife to generously cover the flat dough with the peanut butter. Roll the dough into a log shape, similar to a miniature jelly roll.

Cut into small pieces, ⅓- to ½-inch thick. The final result will be pieces that look like pretty pinwheels.

Angel
Kisses

1/3 cup peanut butter

1 cup sugar

1/2 teaspoon cream of tartar

1/3 cup sour cream

3 tablespoons light corn syrup

Dash salt

2 tablespoons butter or margarine

1 1/2 teaspoons vanilla

2 cups chopped walnuts

Combine the peanut butter, sugar, cream of tartar, sour cream, corn syrup, and salt together in a medium saucepan. Cook on medium-low heat until a soft ball begins to form, or soft-ball stage. The correct stage has been reached when a drop of the mixture forms into a soft ball that slightly flattens when placed in a bowl of cold water.

Continue cooking for 5 minutes, stirring continuously so the mixture doesn't stick to the pan.

Remove from the heat. Add the butter and vanilla and stir well. Cool slightly and fold in the walnuts. Drop by teaspoonful onto wax paper and allow to set before eating.

Peanut
Brittle

2 cups sugar

1 cup light corn syrup

½ cup water

½ cup peanut butter

1 cup margarine or butter

2 cups chopped peanuts

1 teaspoon baking soda

In a large saucepan, heat the sugar, corn syrup, and water until boiling. Add the peanut butter and butter and stir continuously for 2–3 minutes. Add the peanuts and stir constantly until it reaches a hard-ball stage. The correct stage has been reached when a drop of the mixture forms into a ball when placed in a bowl of cold water.

Remove from the heat and quickly stir in the baking soda. Pour over a large baking sheet. Using forks at opposite ends, begin pulling the mixture and lifting it up from the pan. Loosen as soon as possible and break into pieces.

Christmas
Treats

* *Makes approximately 24 candies* *

1 cup peanut butter
1 cup vegan chocolate chips
¾ cup maple syrup

1 cup chopped pecans
1 teaspoon peppermint extract

Heat peanut butter, chocolate chips, and maple syrup in large saucepan until just melted. Fold in pecans and peppermint extract. Cook on medium-low for about 5 minutes.

Transfer to a medium bowl and refrigerate mixture for at least 2 hours. After chilling, roll into bite-size balls.

Dips, Sauces, Toppings, & Spreads

Five-Layer
Dip

2 cups crushed vanilla wafers

1½ cups peanut butter

Water

2 cups trail mix that includes banana chips, coconut, and raisins

1 (9-ounce) package chocolate chips

1 (7-ounce) jar marshmallow cream

Build layers in a 9 x 9-inch dish, beginning with the crushed vanilla wafers.

Microwave the peanut butter in a small microwave-safe bowl, adding a few drops of water in increments in order to make it pourable. This is the next layer.

Sprinkle the trail mix and chocolate chips on top of the peanut butter layer.

Microwave the jar of marshmallow cream for a few seconds to make it pourable and then add it as the final layer of the dip. Serve with large apple slices or unfrosted cookies.

Peanut
Colada Dip

⅓ cup peanut butter

¾ cup milk

1 (8-ounce) can crushed pineapple
  with juice

½ cup sour cream

1 (3.4-ounce) package instant
  coconut pudding mix

Mix all ingredients together in a large bowl until well blended. Refrigerate until ready to serve.

This dip is delicious served with toasted pita chips or sliced fruits. It is also scrumptious as a dessert poured over sweetened rice.

Luscious
Autumn Dip

∗ Makes 1 1/2 cups ∗

¾ cup peanut butter
¾ cup canned pumpkin
½ cup brown sugar

1 tablespoon vanilla
1 teaspoon nutmeg
1 teaspoon cinnamon

Combine ingredients in a medium microwave-safe bowl and heat in microwave for 2 minutes. Stir thoroughly. Serve warm at the table with a tea-light candle, sterno, or low-setting electric fondue pot. Delicious served with slices of pears, apples, carrots, and nut or fruit breads.

Perfect Peanut Butter
Icing

❋ Makes 2 cups ❋

2 cups powdered sugar
1/3 cup smooth peanut butter
2 teaspoons butter or margarine

4 to 6 teaspoons milk
1 teaspoon vanilla

In a small bowl, blend all ingredients and beat with a hand mixer until smooth. Use to frost your favorite cake, cupcake, or cookie.

Fluffy
Dip

½ cup crunchy peanut butter

1 cup sour cream

¼ cup shredded coconut

¼ cup chopped pecans

4 teaspoons crystallized ginger pieces

In a small bowl, combine the peanut butter and sour cream and blend well. Fold in the coconut, pecans, and ginger. This is a wonderful stuffing for cored apples or used as a dip with fancy crackers, pita bread, or naan.

Homemade Peanut Butter
Chocolate Sauce

❋ Makes 2 cups ❋

1 (3-ounce) package chocolate
   pudding mix

1 cup water

⅓ cup peanut butter

¾ cup light corn syrup

In a medium saucepan, combine pudding mix and water and cook on medium high heat. Stir well to remove any lumps and allow to boil until sauce thickens, about 5 minutes.

Remove from heat and add the peanut butter and corn syrup and stir vigorously until smooth. Serve while still warm over ice cream, sundaes, or pound cake.

Peanut Butter
Topping

1 cup brown sugar
$^1/_2$ cup water

$^1/_2$ cup peanut butter
Chopped peanuts, optional

In a small saucepan, combine sugar and water over high heat. Stir constantly and boil for about 2 minutes, until sugar is no longer grainy. Remove from heat and beat in peanut butter until smooth, about 2 minutes. Serve poured over ice cream or frozen treats with a sprinkling of peanuts, if desired.

Cherry
Topping

* *Makes 3 cups* *

⅓ cup quick oats
3 tablespoons flour
3 tablespoons sugar
1 teaspoon cinnamon

2 tablespoons cold butter
⅓ cup peanut butter
1 (15-ounce) can cherry pie filling

In a large bowl, combine the oats, flour, sugar, and cinnamon. Cut in the butter until the mixture is crumbly.

In a medium bowl, stir the peanut butter into the cherry pie filling. Add to the oat mixture and thoroughly combine.

This topping is excellent over baked apples as a side dish. It's also wonderful over baked cobblers or crisps. You can also pour it over a ham before baking.

California
Delight

✱ *Makes 1 heaping cup* ✱

¾ cup peanut butter

⅛ cup orange juice

1 tablespoon grated orange zest

4 tablespoons Nutella spread

¼ cup shredded coconut

3 tablespoons dried cranberries

3 tablespoons crushed banana chips

3 tablespoons candied papaya

Mix all ingredients together in a large bowl and spread generously on banana bread, zucchini bread, or bagels.

Peanut Butter and
Pear Spread

Makes 1³/₄ cups

8 ounces Neufchatel cheese, softened

½ cup chunky peanut butter

3 tablespoons honey

2 tablespoons orange juice

¾ cup chopped pears

½ cup pecan pieces

Combine the cheese, peanut butter, honey, and orange juice in a medium bowl and blend well. Fold in the pears and pecans. Serve on slices of zucchini bread, banana bread, or on bagels or hearty crackers.

Index

Metric Conversion Chart

Volume Measurements		Weight Measurements		Temperature Conversion	
U.S.	Metric	U.S.	Metric	Fahrenheit	Celsius
1 teaspoon	5 ml	½ ounce	15 g	250	120
1 tablespoon	15 ml	1 ounce	30 g	300	150
¼ cup	60 ml	3 ounces	90 g	325	160
⅓ cup	75 ml	4 ounces	115 g	350	180
½ cup	125 ml	8 ounces	225 g	375	190
⅔ cup	150 ml	12 ounces	350 g	400	200
¾ cup	175 ml	1 pound	450 g	425	220
1 cup	250 ml	2¼ pounds	1 kg	450	230